First Time Home Buyer Gu de: The Basics of Investing in Real Estate by Lenzi Hudson

Self-Published by Kindle Direct Publishing

The advice and strategies found within may not be suitable for every situation. This work is sold with the understanding that neither the author nor the publisher are held responsible for the results accrued from the advice in this book.

© 2021 Lenzi Hudson.

All rights reserved. No portion of this book may be reproduced in any form without permission from the publisher, except as permitted by U.S. copyright law. For permissions contact:

Cover by Pixasquare on Unsplash.

TABLE OF CONTENTS

- **1** INTRODUCTION
- **2** RELATIONSHIP WITH YOUR REALTOR
- **4** PRE-APPROVAL
- **5** CREDIT
- **7** INVESTING
- **12** MORTGAGE LENDER
- **14** LOANS
- **19** THE SEARCH
- **23** THE OFFER
- **25** UNDER CONTRACT
- **32** CLOSING
- **35** CONCLUSION

LENZI HUDSON
REALTOR®

I would like to start off by introducing myself. I am Lenzi Hudson. I am a Real Estate Agent in Denver, Colorado. I've always had a passion for building generational wealth and reaching financial freedom. My dad introduced me to stocks in college, and that was the moment I fell in love with the idea of making passive income.

I had the opportunity of living in California where I graduated from the Fashion Institute of Design and Merchandising with a focus in Merchandising & Marketing. Through this experience, living in Downtown L.A. gave me the confidence to work in fast-paced environments and comfort in being uncomfortable, enhancing my ability to think on my feet, and made me fall in love with getting to connect with so many amazing people. While I had an unforgettable experience, my appreciation for my hometown has grown and I'm excited to be back.

My passion comes to fruition when I'm creating experiences and developing long-lasting relationships. I believe both are imperative for success in real estate. Purchasing a home or even investing in real estate is an impactful milestone in everyone's life. My love of serving others and my infatuation of beautiful architecture makes this the perfect career for me. I would love and be honored to be a part of making your dreams and "happy place" a reality by introducing you to the basics of investing in real estate!

INTRODUCTION

There is a massive misconception of purchasing your first home. False claims linger over the newly graduated college class and others that have been stuck under the safety net of renting. Subconsciously, you believe that it's extremely difficult to purchase a home and that you must be in the best of the best financial situations just to be given an opportunity to make an offer on a home you've fallen in love with. Erase all of that nonsense from your brain and let's start fresh. I will lay down the facts and foundation of being a First Time Home Buyer. I am here to clear the stigmas that are clouding your vision from the real process of investing in real estate. Let's begin by explaining the importance of your relationship with your Real Estate Agent.

RELATIONSHIP WITH YOUR REALTOR

Choosing a real estate agent is just as important as if you were choosing a therapist to work with. Believe it or not, the process of searching for a home is an emotional one. For all of you who don't believe that, I want you to close your eyes and imagine finding a condo with a perfect view, it's in your price range, and is in a favorable radius to your job and favorite hangout spots. One might call this a dream situation. You finally listen to your intuition to put your offer on a home, but the listing agent replies saying the sellers just accepted another offer. Heartbreaking, I know; that's what I'm here for. When it's time to let out every concern and anxiety provoking worry during the process, your agent is your go-to person, your 24/7 problem solver, and your professional home scout. Fiduciary, describes this type of relationship.

<u>FIDUCIARY</u> (NOUN)

AN AGENT THAT ACTS ON BEHALF OF THEIR PRINCIPLE, PUTTING THEIR CLIENTS' INTEREST ABOVE THEIR OWN, WITH A DUTY TO PRESERVE GOOD FAITH AND TRUST.

The term fiduciary exemplifies the duty the agent has of having the principle's (your) best interest and holding it above everyone else's. Your agent promises to make any and every decision with your best interest. They commit to keeping your personal information confidential, to disclose all material facts they discover, and to refrain from representing an opposing party in the transaction. It's a misconception that realtors are interested in knowing their Buyer's and or Seller's financial situations. This is far from the truth! Agents recommend that Buyers discuss and evaluate their financial status with a mortgage lender. After meeting with your lender, you will be informed on how much house you can actually afford, as well as the steps you can take to improve your credit score or LTV ratio. Communication is key during the home searching process. Agents are constantly on the search for the newest listings. Expect to get texts frequently from your Agent regarding updates on the current listings. The real estate world is constantly changing. Homes leave the market just as fast as they're listed. If your agent isn't responsive or on top of their communication, RUN! Find an agent that you trust, that listens to you, and has your best interest in mind. Only work with an agent who will put you on track to reach a smooth closing and increase your peace of mind. You shouldn't have to worry about your needs being met.

THE PRE-APPROVAL

A pre-approval letter is like putting the key into the ignition. The home buying process should always start by you scheduling an appointment with your lender to get a clear idea of your shopping budget. This letter confirms the amount of money you can afford to spend on purchasing a home. Briefly, your lender should address what your monthly payments and interest rate will look like.

WHY THIS LETTER IS SO NECESSARY:

Going home shopping without a pre-approval letter is like going grocery shopping without enough money... You get to the checkout, or in this case closing date and someone has to break the news to you, "Sorry honey, but you can't afford all that." Talk about a heartbreak. Consulting with a lender not only discloses what you really have to work with, but it also saves you and your lender's time from finding an amazing home that is not in your financial league. In addition to saving you and your agent's time, the sellers also want to know that you're a serious candidate from their end of the deal. If and when it comes down to the sellers choosing which offer they'll accept, more often than not, they'll choose the buyer who is pre-approved over a buyer who is not. They need confirmation that you can actually pay them when the time arises.

LET'S TALK CREDIT SCORE

For those who don't already know, your credit score is your financial report card. This number ranks you by the risk of your past money making decisions, and whether or not you have proved to consistently pay your bills on time. Your credit score is a three-digit number that ranges from 300 to 850. 300 being poor credit and 850 putting you in the top tier with all of the crystal clear credit score holders. Don't downplay the importance of raising your credit score. This is how you will earn and keep a lender's attention. They need to believe that they can trust you with their money.

Your credit score affects your ability to qualify for certain loans, and influences the percent of the sales price you'll need as the down payment that you'll put towards the home. According to FHA.com, to qualify to put a down payment of 3.5%, you must hold a credit score of 580 or higher. Any score falling below the 580 benchmark, must put at least 10% down on a house to qualify on the FHA loan.

CREDIT REPORT

A credit report displays the story of your credit history. It discloses each and every situation where you've borrowed money, whether or not you've made your payments on time, and it also influences a lender's decision on their comfortability of letting you borrow from them. In addition, your credit report helps determine how much they'll lend you, and what rate you'll have on your monthly mortgage payments. It is imperative to develop the habit of checking your credit report annually to resolve any errors that may arise. Errors may result in you having a higher interest rate. Let's avoid that at all costs! You can request a free credit report from Experian.com. Monitoring your credit report may also help spot any type of fraud or theft that could be used against you. The more aware you are of any issues that arise, the sooner you'll be able to solve them.

WEALTHY HABITS

TIPS ON BUILDING YOUR SAVINGS

Creating a home buying budget and keeping track of all the money you've earned, down to the cent, is essential when saving up for a home... let alone the down payment. It's necessary to know exactly where your money is going. Without a clear vision, it's impossible to determine where your actions are taking you. Don't be blind when it comes to your financial decisions. You may be steering yourself in the wrong direction. First and foremost--and I say this with all the love in my heart-- pay off your loans and do NOT acquire anymore. As soon as you're free of your debt, you can save more and reach your home buying goals sooner. I promise you, it'll be worth it in the long run.

Next, write down your list of non-negotiable items that you need to account for each month. This includes your current rent, student loan payment, car payment, gas, toiletries...etc. This list is made up of the different financial responsibilities that you're held accountable for. A simple saving tactic that I've had success with is living below my means.

Yes, we've all heard this saying before, but I mean it! Live in your current financial lifestyle. Your home savings account is begging you to eat at home and to stop making impulsive buying decisions on stuff you don't need. This means you are going to master saying "No." to going out to get drinks every weekend, and buying unnecessary items that won't lead you towards a quicker start date for your home search. When you're tempted on buying something outside of your budget, think of all the extra money you can have to put towards closing costs or investing in the furniture to decorate your new place. I will always be an advocate of living in the moment, but with finances, I recommend focusing on the bigger picture. The quicker you change your spending habits, the faster you can afford your dream home, which means you can start building equity sooner.

WHY YOU SHOULD INVEST NOW!

It's wise to invest in a home and skip the renting phase, because you are throwing your money away whenever you aren't investing in yourself or your future. Why pay someone else, when you can use that same amount to put towards your own investment? No matter the angle you look at home owning, it'll always benefit you more than renting.

OWNERSHIP GAINS

EQUITY (NOUN)

THE DIFFERENCE BETWEEN HOW MUCH YOU HAVE LEFT TO PAY TOWARDS YOUR MORTGAGE AND HOW MUCH YOUR HOME IS CURRENTLY WORTH.

The value of your home naturally increases over time; your house appreciates as the market goes through changes.

Here are a few ways to gain equity faster (in your home):
- Make a larger down payment
- Pay more than the required monthly payments
- Home improvements can increase home value

WHAT IS AN ASSET?

There are three categories an asset can fall under: real, financial, or intangible. Real estate is considered a real asset. "Real" in terms of the asset being tangible. According to Investopedia, "real asset" is defined as, "a tangible investment that has an intrinsic value due to its substance and physical properties.". An asset is where the value can be exchanged for cash. Other examples of real assets that are tangible include pieces of gold, machinery, and oil.

WHAT IS A
LIABILITY?

Would this really be considered an investment guide if I didn't define what a liability is? Absolutely not. A liability is an obligation where you owe someone money and you've promised to pay them back. Oh honey, you'll pay them back all right. Actually, you will end up paying way more than what you originally owed, when that interest comes into play. The most common liabilities are buying brand new cars, paying rent, agreeing to long term bank loans... etc. When I began dipping my toe into the investing world, the first statement imprinted into my mind was, "Assets over Liabilities. You should have an asset that can cover every liability." Re-read that a couple times, until it clicks. It's just a change of perspective. If you have an asset that covers the cost of your dream car and all the clothes you could ever dream of, you're not spending any of your income that you're actually laboring for. This means you have more money to save or invest into more rental properties and stocks.

ASSET
LIABILITY

In order to have equity and not owe anyone money, it's necessary that you own an asset that is increasing in value. This advance in value can be exchanged for money. The money you've earned, or the increase of value gained on an asset you own, is considered passive income.

PASSIVE INCOME

You've all heard it before, "I make money in my sleep.". I don't know about you, but I've always wanted to say that subtle flex for sure. Passive income is earned with little to no active effort being made. You can receive passive income through owning a rental property, investing in stocks, vending machines, laundromats... you get the idea. Money is consistently made by someone's reoccurring necessity of the item, product, or service that is being offered.

PASSIVE INCOME = FINANCIAL FREEDOM

Financial freedom is met when you create multiple streams of passive income. It's like a gift that keeps giving. Seven streams of income is proven to bring you to financial freedom. This isn't something that happens overnight. Stay focused and create money-making opportunities for yourself. Becoming financially free is very possible, and you are deserving of just that!

FINDING A MORTGAGE LENDER

Questions to Ask:

What amount do I qualify for to borrow towards purchasing a home?

To come up with this amount, the mortgage lender will consider the amount of debt you currently have, and they'll review your credit history. Furthermore, they'll check your employment status and evaluate the difference between your annual income and the amount of debt you're committed to.

How much money do I need to put towards my Down Payment?

Your down payment affects your mortgage interest rate percentage and what your monthly payments will amount to.

How many discount points does my rate include?

A discount point is paid to your lender in exchange for a reduced interest rate.

1 discount point = 1% lower interest rate

FINDING A MORTGAGE LENDER

Questions to Ask:

What are my estimated closing costs?

This is important to note when creating your budget. Closing costs are additional fees you must pay when finalizing the process of purchasing a home. Your lender will be able to provide you a Good Faith estimate breaking down what your estimated closing costs will be.

What will the interest rate be?

Ask your Lender for an interest rate quote, in addition to your APR (Annual Percentage Rate) for your loan. I recommend that you receive three quotes from three different lenders. Having options allows for you to make an educated decision. Once you compare all three, the quote that makes the most sense for your situation will be more apparent to you because you have a breakdown of what each lender is offering you. Don't commit until you see all of your options. You should feel comfortable with your decision because you will be committed to it for awhile.

Once you decide on a lender, make sure to introduce them to your real estate agent. They will need to be in contact for the duration of the home buying process.

LOANS

Let's review National Loan Programs that make it possible to get a mortgage with low credit scores or limited down payment. Before I begin to dissect the various loan options you have, I have a few things I want to go over. Depending on the type of loan you choose (Conventional, VA or FHA) and your credit score, you can put as low as 3-3.5% for the down payment. I encourage Buyers to put the most they can afford down, so they don't have to commit to borrowing more money than they have to. I'd say to aim for the 20%. Putting down 20% will not only make you more appealing to your lender, but you'll also reduce extra fees you'll have added to your monthly mortgage payments.

But First...

LET'S DISCUSS

INTEREST RATE

Interest rate is influenced upon market fluctuations. During the process of obtaining a loan, your lender will inform you on your set interest rate as well as notify you of the cost of your monthly payments. This is very important information to know! If you don't feel well-informed or comfortable with your rates or payments, it's imperative to compare rates to other lenders you could work with. It's a big commitment, don't rush.

DOWNPAYMENT

A down payment, is the money you will pay out of pocket towards purchasing a home. This amount, is contingent upon your financial situation and your house shopping budget. The more money you can pay upfront, the less money you'll have to borrow and pay interest on. Aim to pay 20% of the sales price of the home. By paying 20%, you will avoid having to pay for Private Mortgage Insurance.

PRIVATE MORTGAGE INSURANCE

If you put a down payment below 20% of the sales price of the home, you're going to have to pay for private mortgage insurance (PMI). Private Mortgage Insurance protects your lender if you end up making a default on the loan. PMI is required from conventional mortgage lenders. Once you reach 20% equity- either through paying down your loan or if your house rises in value- or your loan balance reaches 80% of the home's original value, you can contact your lender to remove the PMI from your mortgage payments. PMI payments can range between $30-$70 per $100,000 you borrow. The higher your credit score the lower your PMI rate will be. So it's a pro to put 20% down if you can, to avoid the extra payments

••

Depending on your financial situation and the date you're planning to close on your new home, you may not be able to put the full 20% down. As a First Time Home Buyer, you're able to take advantage of the opportunity of lower down payments. The option of a lower down payment gives more people the opportunity to get a house sooner. This is beneficial especially since you'll have so much to pay for at once. Also, the lower down payment percentages allows you to have more savings to fall back on if needed. Evaluate your financial situation and see which option is the most favorable to you.

Conventional Loans

Conventional Loans are best when seeking a low down payment and limited mortgage insurance premiums. This type of loan isn't backed up by the government, meaning the requirements may be stricter to qualify. First Time Home Buyers can get a conventional loan with as little as 3% for the down payment. Remember, if you put 20% down towards the house, you will not be required to pay for private mortgage insurance, which will be tied in with your monthly mortgage payments. Think of it like this, the more money you put down, the less money you'll owe every month. To qualify for a conventional loan, a credit score of 620 is typically required. Once your credit score soars to the higher end towards 720, you can benefit by receiving better interest rates that ultimately affect how much you'll owe each month. In other words, get your credit score up! In addition to your credit score, it's important to analyze your Debt-to-Income (DTI) ratio. A simple way to put it, your debt-to-income refers to your current total amount of debt you have. This is your car payment, student loans, rent...etc.) divided by your monthly income before tax. To figure out your DTI percentage, there are several DTI calculators you can find online. Typically lenders require 36% or lower to qualify for a conventional loan.

FHA Loans

FHA stands for Federal Housing Administration. FHA loans are best for buyers who have a lower credit score and are looking for a lower down payment. This loan type is supported by the government which means that lenders are more lenient with your financial history. Credit scores of 580 or higher qualify the buyer to put a down payment as low as 3.5%. If your credit score falls below 500, you must put a minimum of 10% of the sales price for the down payment. Remember, and I can't stress this enough, if your down payment doesn't reach 20% of the sales price you will be required to pay additional PMI fees.

VA Loans

VA loans are developed by the United States Department of Veterans Administration. Take advantage of this loan if you're a veteran or family of someone who is. VA loans are a gem to take advantage of if you qualify. You won't be required to make a down payment. In addition, you won't be responsible for mortgage insurance, prepayment penalties, and you will have limited costs to cover at closing.

• •

Take time to research First Time Home Buyer Programs that are offered in the state you live in or are deciding to purchase in! Each program may have different requirements to qualify!

THE SEARCH

In my opinion, the search is the most fun out of the entire process, next to closing, of course. What does your 'happy place' look like? Make sure you are aware of what you're looking for beforehand. This will benefit your time as well as your agent's time. The homes that don't match your requirements can immediately get weeded out of the list of choices. Once that happens, the majority of your time can be used to schedule showings on houses you know you'll love.

WHAT ARE YOU LOOKING FOR?

ANSWER THESE QUESTIONS

WHAT IS YOUR TIMEFRAME ON MOVING?
- DO YOU NEED A QUICK CLOSE?
- IS YOUR MOVING DATE CONTINGENT ON AN EXISTING LEASE END DATE?

TOWNHOUSE, CONDO, SINGLE FAMILY, DUPLEX?
ARE YOU OPEN TO CHECKING OUT MULTIPLE PROPERTY TYPES, OR ARE YOU LOCKED IN ON ONE SPECIFIC TYPE OF PROPERTY?

WHAT IS YOUR PRICE RANGE?
- YOUR PRICE RANGE SHOULD BE BASED OFF OF YOUR PRE-APPROVED LOAN AMOUNT AND HOW MUCH YOU'RE ABLE TO PUT DOWN AT CLOSING.
- THINK ABOUT HOW MUCH YOU CAN AFFORD TO PAY MONTHLY. (CONSIDERING YOUR OTHER BILLS)
- INCLUDE HOA FEES WHEN DETERMINING YOUR BUDGET.

WHAT LOCATION/AREAS DO YOU PREFER?
- DO YOU WANT TO BE IN A 5 MILE RADIUS FROM YOUR JOB?
- DO YOU WANT TO BE CLOSE TO YOUR FRIENDS AND FAMILY?
- DO YOU PREFER THE SUBURBS OR THE CITY?

HOW MANY BEDROOMS & BATHROOMS?
DO YOU WANT A GUEST BEDROOM?

SCHEDULING TIME FOR SHOWINGS

ONCE YOUR AGENT UNDERSTANDS WHAT YOU'RE LOOKING FOR, THEY WILL SEND YOU THE PROPERTIES THAT MATCH THOSE REQUIREMENTS AS THEY POP UP ON THE MARKET. IN THE CURRENT MARKET OF JANUARY 2021, HOUSES ARE NOT STAYING ACTIVE ON THE MARKET FOR LONG, SO IT'S CRITICAL TO SCHEDULE SHOWINGS AS SOON AS YOU'VE EXPRESSED INTEREST. YOU MUST MAKE TIME TO VIEW THE HOUSES IN PERSON. PICTURES DON'T GIVE THE HOME THE JUSTICE IT DESERVES. THESE SHOWINGS SHOULD BE A PRIORITY DURING THE SEARCHING PROCESS BECAUSE IF YOU'RE NOT GOING TO SEE THE HOME, SOMEONE ELSE IS. I'D SAY TO DEDICATE 2 DAYS A WEEK TO CHECK OUT HOMES THAT HAVE THE POTENTIAL TO BE WINNERS! SHOWINGS ARE TYPICALLY 15-30 MINUTES.

DON'T MAKE EMOTIONAL DECISIONS

The home shopping experience is a very emotional one. You can potentially fall in love with a home and it'll get stripped away from you from one counteroffer. It's important to keep a positive attitude throughout the process, and try to practice non-attachment. The house isn't yours until you've received the keys at closing. My point is, don't purchase a home based off of your emotions. This life changing decision should only be made off of logic and looking at the big picture

THE BIG PICTURE:

- Potential equity growth.
- Monthly payments, in addition to your other monthly financial responsibilities.
- What life will be like in the area you choose- money spent on gas neighborhood you'll be in, etc.

THE OFFER

Depending on the housing market, it will typically lean towards being more of a beneficial transaction for the sellers or for the buyers. In the first quarter of 2021, it's a seller's market. The seller is in a favorable position for many reasons; The inventory of homes for sale are low, which increases the demand for buyers. This high demand of buyer's wanting to purchase a home, gives a seller the ability to charge more than what their home is actually worth. In this market, sellers are accepting offers 2% from the sales price. Any offer below 2% of what the Sellers are asking for may knock you down a few levels when it comes to accepting your offer.

- If you were to receive a call that another Buyer submitted an offer that was $1,000 more than you and it was accepted, how would you feel?
- Does my offer reflect my interest in this home?
- Can I afford this home?

These questions bring reality into play when determining your offer price. If a house completely won you over, why are you not comfortable offering the full listing price on the home? Don't get me wrong, if you don't have that amount in your budget, it's still worth a try to see if you can come out on top, by offering what you do have available. Especially with the current market in January 2021, houses are not staying on the market for long. If a house is a 10/10 in your eyes, make sure your offer reflects that.

CLOSING DATE?

Once your agent has your offer price, they have a couple other things they'll need to know when writing out the contract. One question your agent will ask is your preferred closing date. This date should have a buffer. In a real estate transaction, dates and deadlines can change at any time with an Amend-Extend contract. The average days it takes to close on a home is 30-45 days; a month to a month and a half.

THE WAIT.

This is the time to meditate and take your mind away from real estate and your dream home until you find out if your offer has been accepted or if the Sellers are sending a counteroffer that you will need to respond to. Your Agent will add an acceptance date and time, of when they need to have the Seller's decision. Typically, this will be at some point during the following day.

COUNTEROFFER

It's not surprsing to submit an offer and receive a counteroffer in return. A counteroffer is the Seller's response to your offer. Your offer is rejected, and they replace it with their updated version. Anything from a price change, different dates/deadlines, to the request of an appraisal gap could be addressed in the counteroffer. Once you receive the counteroffer you have three options:

1. You can accept the Seller's offer.
2. You can reject the Seller's offer.
3. You can send back another counteroffer.

UNDER CONTRACT

Once your contract is signed by the Listing Agent and the Seller, your Agent will send you the great news! This means that the Buyer (you) and Seller have agreed on all of the terms addressed; you're officially under contract.

LET THE PROCESS BEGIN!

Yay, your offer got accepted and you are now officially under contract. Now what?

IMPORTANCE OF DATES & DEADLINES

You are aware that deadlines are important to meet. In real estate, dates and deadlines are "time is of the essence". This means that these are definite dates and times that need to be met or there are consequences. For example, if your Buyer Agent is requesting your Earnest Money and you don't end up making the deadline, your contract is void. You lost the house.

•••••••••••••••••••••••••••••••••

Your agent will make sure you receive a copy of the executed contract. Make sure you mark your calendar with all of the dates to ensure that you will be able meet all of the deadlines. Stay aware of what needs to be done and what documents you will need to get back to your agent, as well as your mortgage lender.

The contract's first deadline will be your agent turning in your earnest money check.

EARNEST MONEY

Earnest money is proof to the Seller that you have serious intentions and interest in purchasing their home. The Seller may have a minimum amount of earnest money they're requesting to hold. Once the earnest money is collected, this is when the house is no longer active on all of the real estate searching sites, and it will appear as "pending". This check is held by the title company you're working with. You can find this requested amount by asking your Agent. At the end of closing, you will have your earnest money returned to you in full. There are a few scenarios I'd like to address where you could lose your earnest money:

- If you waive your contingencies, which is your protection as a buyer.

For example, you decided to waive your contingencies; if the mortgage falls through or something goes wrong with your inspection and you want to back out of the contract... kiss that earnest money goodbye. Make sure you fully understand what you're getting yourself into before signing that contract.

- Not meeting the dates/deadlines in the contract will have you forfeit your earnest money check.
- If you decide to back out and it had nothing to do with any financial issues or the inspection, you've just lost your earnest money honey.

THE INSPECTION

Next, you will be given the choice to have a general home inspection scheduled. This is highly recommended but not required. The purpose of an inspection, is to ensure that everything beyond the surface (that your eyes cannot see), is brought to your attention. For example, a home inspection will uncover what condition the roof and gutters are in and the water pressure will be checked to reveal any leaks. These are just a few things that you will have inspected. Once you're aware of the different things that need to be fixed and or resolved, your agent will create an Inspection Objection. This is a list of requests that will be forwarded to the Sellers to fix. In the contract, under dates and deadlines, there will a date for an Inspection Resolution. This specific date is when the Sellers need every request you've listed on the Inspection Objection resolved. If you're not pleased with their efforts on getting these things fixed, you have the right to back out of the contract. In addition to a general home inspection, your agent will recommend a radon test and sewage scope.

Home Warranty

A home warranty is a temporary insurance on your appliances and any service mentioned in the specific plan you choose. A home can very well come with a home warranty if negotiated in the contract. Every situation is different. Home warranties also vary in length of time; there are 1 year, 3 year, 5 year... Once they expire, you are allowed to extended or renew your warranty.

Fun Fact: *New Construction homes come with a 1 Year Workmanship and a 10 Year Structural Warranty by default.*

APPRAISAL

Now it's time for the appraisal. Your lender is in charge of ordering the appraisal, and the listing agent is responsible for scheduling it. An appraisal, is an estimate of the value of the property, provided by an expert. The listing price is reflected by the Seller's opinion of what they think their house is currently worth. The appraisal displays the actual value. In some cases, the Seller may ask you if you're willing to include an appraisal gap clause, and for how much. There is a possibility that the Seller is not certain that their appraisal will match the listing price, that's what the appraisal gap is for.

APPRAISAL GAP GUARANTEE CLAUSE:

This clause states that if the home were to appraise lower than the stated purchase price, the buyer would bring money above appraised value OR make up the entire difference between the appraised value and purchase price. For example, let's say the house you're buying is $500,000 and you agreed on a $10,000 appraisal gap. If the home appraises undervalue at $460,000, you'll add the $10,000 gap and end up paying $470,000 instead.

SURVEY

Next, the Title company you're working with will send documents over for you to review and sign. After reviewing the documents, you will know if they'll require you to order a survey or a ILC (Improvement Location Certificate).

A survey will be a document that shows all of your property lines that you own versus what you don't own. This is important to be aware of, in order to avoid any encroachments that could result in liens being added to the property. An encroachment is when you build or add something to your property, such as a driveway or fencing, and it hangs over your property onto someone else's property. This is where a lien can get added onto your property. You're required to correct the situation.

CLOSING

After signing several other contracts, and reading endless HOA documents, you've finally reached the finish line! Don't celebrate just yet. You must turn over your closing costs which include:

- Loan (origination, discount, and application fee)
- Inspection (General Home Inspection, Radon Test, & Sewage Scope)
- Appraisal
- Private Mortgage Insurance Premiums
- Title Search + Title Insurance
- Homeowner's Hazard Insurance

These are a few costs that may be a part of your closing fees. Each closing is different, just as each contract holds it's own negotiated word. Your lender will prepare you with a Good Faith Estimate.

A **Good Faith Estimate** is a calculated estimate of what you will be expected to bring to closing.

It's important that you review your contract and make sure all of your costs match what you initially negotiated. It's between the Buyer and Seller to decide who pays what, or if they're deciding to split the costs halfway.

CLOSING DATE VS. POSSESSION DATE

Closing day means it's time to collect the keys to your new home!! You'll notice on your contract, under the dates and deadlines, a spot labeled 'Closing Date', and right beneath that, there is another spot labeled 'Possession Date'. Depending on what's been negotiated, these dates could definitely be the same day, or even a couple days a part.

Possession Date means you already have the deed to your home; you've allowed the Seller's a couple extra days to remove the rest of their possessions and fully leave the house vacant and move-in ready. It's important to add a fee if the Sellers are still living in the sold home beyond their expired Possession Date. For example, you can charge the Seller $150 per night they extend their stay in the home. This late fee induces the Seller's urgency to move out.

TYPES OF DEEDS

GENERAL WARRANTY DEED- THE GRANTOR IS STATING THAT THEY'RE TRANSFERRING OWNERSHIP OF THE PROPERTY TO THE GRANTEE (YOU). THIS TYPE OF DEED HAS THE GREATEST AMOUNT OF PROTECTION. IT WARRANTS THAT YOU OWN THE PROPERTY AND THAT IT'S FREE OF ANY LIENS, MORTGAGES, AND ENCUMBRANCES. IF THERE IS A BREACH IN THE WARRANTY, THE SELLER MUST TAKE CARE OF THE SITUATION. IT'S A GENEROUS SIZED RISK TO THE SELLER, BUT MAJOR SECURITY FOR THE BUYER.

SPECIAL WARRANTY DEED- THIS DEED DOESN'T PROTECT THE BUYER AS MUCH AS THE GENERAL WARRANTY DEED, AS IT ONLY CONTAINS TWO WARRANTIES:

- GRANTOR ADDRESSES THAT THEY'VE RECEIVED THE TITLE.
- GRANTOR WARRANTS THAT THERE WERE NO ENCUMBRANCES TO THEIR ACTUAL KNOWLEDGE WHEN THEY HAD OWNERSHIP OF THE PROPERTY.

Conclusion

Now that I've broken down the basics of the homebuying process, I hope you've come to a realization that home ownership is more accessible than you've assumed. Dedicate time each month to evaluate your plan and budget, and make changes when needed. Like I've mentioned before, this is not a quick process. Everyone won't be starting at square one, so it's imperative to have tunnel vision and focus on YOUR situation. Starting your journey today will get you to your home buying goals sooner than you think. Have faith in yourself. Find accountability partners that you can meet with every couple of months to ensure you're on track with your goals.

The five things you should make a priority (in no specific order):
1. Pay off all debt/loans.
2. Increase your credit score.
3. Build up your savings.
4. Meet with three different lenders.
5. Find Accountability Partners.

THIS IS A VERY BIG AND SPECIAL MOMENT IN YOUR LIFE. Ownership is the key to building equity. This will help you establish generationa wealth over time; which you can leave behind for your family. Your home can be passed down to your children one day. Now that's goals!

I want to say thank you for investing into my First Time Home Buyer Guide. It honestly means the world to me. I am passionate about real estate and investing, and I believe it's imperative that you're prepared when the opportunity arises. START INVESTING in yourself and your future, you deserve it and your future self will thank you!

I WOULD LOVE TO WORK WITH YOU & assist you in every step of your home buying journey. I would love and be honored to be a part of making your 'happy place' a reality. I appreciate ALL of the support and EVERY referral you send me!

Be a blessing to your friends and family by sharing this guide with them! Iron sharpens iron.

Lastly, I would appreciate if you could leave an honest review on Amazon of what you think of this guide.

REFERENCES

Braverman, Beth. "Ouch! 3 Times You Can Kiss Your Earnest Money Refund Goodbye>." Real Estate News and Advice | Realtor.com®, Realtor.com, 5 Jan. 2020, www.realtor.com/advice/buy/here-are-3-times-when-can-kiss-your-earnest-money-goodbye/.

Chen, James. "Real Asset: A Tangible Investment." Investopedia, Investopedia, 28 Aug. 2020, www.investopedia.com/terms/r/ .

Chen, James. "What Is a Warranty Deed?" Investopedia, Investopedia, 16 Dec. 2020, www.investopedia.com/terms/w/warranty-deed.asp.

"Colorado Housing and Finance Authority Lenders of 2020." NerdWallet, 16 Nov. 2020, www.nerdwallet.com/best/mortgages/chfa-colorado-housing-finance-authority-lenders.

Credit Requirements for an FHA Loan in 2020, www.fha.com/fha_credit_requirements.

Daigle, Elizabeth. "Escalation Clauses & Appraisal Gap Guarantees." Liz Daigle Real Estate, 20 Feb. 2018, lizdaigle.com/escalation-clauses-appraisal-gaps/.

Dixon, Amanda. "Steps to Building Equity in Your Home." SmartAsset, SmartAsset, 20 Dec. 2016, smartasset.com/mortgage/steps-to-building-equity.

Hayes, Adam. "Liability." Investopedia, Investopedia, 21 Oct. 2020, www.investopedia.com/terms/l/liability.asp.

Kagan, Julia. "Credit Score." Investopedia, Investopedia, 3 Dec. 2020, www.investopedia.com/terms/c/credit_score.asp.

Kielar, Hanna. "11 Ways To Save For A House: Tips & Tricks." 11 Ways To Save For A House: Tips & Tricks | Rocket Mortgage, 23 Oct. 2020, www.rocketmortgage.com/learn/how-to-save-for-a-house.

LaMance, Ken. "Real Estate Agent Liability: Breach of Fiduciary Duty." LegalMatch Law Library, LegalMatch, 11 May 2018, www.legalmatch.com/law-library/article/real-estate-agent-liability-breach-of-fiduciary-duty.html.

Marquand, Barbara. "14 Tips for First-Time Home Buyers." NerdWallet, 9 Dec. 2020, www.nerdwallet.com/article/mortgages/tips-for-first-time-home-buyers.
Resources.display. "Credit Report Basics." Experian, Experian, 23 Aug. 2019, www.experian.com/blogs/ask-experian/credit-education/report-basics/.

Vohwinkle, Jeremy. "The Hidden Cost of Home Ownership Most Buyers Forget." The Balance, 28 July 2020, www.thebalance.com/be-prepared-for-closing-costs-1289841.

Wichter, Zach. "First-Time Homebuyer Loans And Programs." Bankrate, 7 Aug. 2020, www.bankrate.com/mortgages/first-time-homebuyer-loans-and-programs/.

Background images- https://unsplash.com

www.ingramcontent.com/pod-product-compliance
Lightning Source LLC
Chambersburg PA
CBHW040335220526
45473CB00009B/2697